The Moon that Holds us

a story of healing and connection

By

Britney Shawstad
& all of my littles inside

i

Dedication

To Terri,

For guiding me through the journey of healing my parts. Your love and dedication to your profession have been my light, no matter what, and this book carries forward the warmth and wisdom you have shared with me.

To My Husband,

For his unwavering support and unconditional love.

To My Children,

May you always feel safe to share your feelings and know that every part of you is good.

And to Myself and all of my parts,

I vow to always listen to you, hold you with compassion, and love you beyond measure. I am proud of you.

About the Author

Britney Shawstad is a wife, mother, and Marketing and Digital Design professional who has journeyed through her own path of healing with the support of her therapist, Terri. Through her poetic and tender storytelling, she captures the essence of emotional connection, inner child work, and the power of healing. Britney's work is inspired by her own experiences, her love for nature, and the deep bond she shares with her family. She hopes to inspire others to look within and find comfort in their own journeys of self-compassion and love. Britney resides in Everett, Washington, with her three kids, husband Garrett, and dog Atlas.

In addition to writing, Britney has developed the Calming Triggers app, a simple and practical tool designed to support navigating triggers. With its easy-to-use interface, the app helps users identify and utilize coping tools, providing a gentle, empowering way to find calm in moments of overwhelm. Learn more and download the Calming Triggers App: calmingtriggers.com

"The Moon That Holds Us " is a celebration of the healing journey and the enduring power of connection, even in the darkest of times.

Table of Contents

In a cozy home, lived Britney with her three little ones, Harrison, Lowen, and Aspen. They loved hearing stories about how everyone has different parts inside them. These parts are like a little family, each with their own job.

"Inside me, inside you, there are many different parts," Britney began. "Some parts are like helpers who try to keep us safe; some are playful and like to have fun, and others might feel scared or sad. Sometimes, these parts inside me need help, just like when you need me to listen to you or give you a hug."

"When my parts feel confused or upset," Britney continued, "I go see someone very special – her name is Terri. She helps me learn about my parts, how they feel and how to take care of them."

"Who is Terri?" asked Lowen with wide eyes.

"Terri is my therapist, she is like a guide," Britney explained. "She helps me listen to the little parts inside me. Like 'little baby Britney,' who feels scared and lonely sometimes, and 'brave Britney,' who tries to protect me to keep me safe. It's like when you get upset or nervous, and I help you feel better. Terri shows me how to listen to my parts so they know they're safe and don't have to worry so much."

"One day," said Britney, "my little parts were very scared because Terri was going on a break. They worried, just like you might when you go to school or I leave for a little while."

"Terri told me something magical," whispered Britney. "She said we could look at the moon while we are apart. Whenever I felt lonely or scared, I could look up at the moon, it would be our reminder that we are thinking of each other and my little parts will never feel alone."

"The moon?" Harrison asked, eyes wide with surprise.

"Yes," Britney smiled. "Even when we're apart, the moon is always there, shining down on us and reminding us we are still loved even when we are apart. That love does not go away when we are not together."

"Sometimes, when my parts feel scared inside, like little baby Britney, or get tired of being strong, like brave Britney," Britney said gently. "When that happens, Terri taught me to remind them they're not alone. I can take care of them with Terri's help, just like I take care of you."

"What happens when she goes on breaks?" Lowen asked.

"So when Terri goes on her breaks, she told me to look at the moon," Britney continued. "It's our special reminder that we are still connected, even when we are apart. It's like how you can feel my love when I am not in the room with you." Lowen smiled.

"Terri once told me," Britney said softly, "That I have the strength to care for all of my parts, even when it feels hard. She helps me practice, reminding me that just like the moon lights up the sky, I can bring light to the parts inside me, too."

Lowen asked, "Do I have parts inside me too?"

"You have little parts inside you, too," Britney said softly. "Sometimes, one part of you might feel like crying while another part wants to be brave. And that's okay."

"Just like I care for my parts," Britney smiled, "it is my duty as your mom to care for yours. I can listen to you, hold you close, and always remind you that you are safe."

"And whenever you feel sad or miss mommy, just look at the moon," Britney said. "Know that my love is always shining down on you and that you are never alone."

"You know," said Harrison thoughtfully, "I know Terri is really special to you, Mommy."

Britney nodded, her heart swelling with love. "She is. She has helped me and my parts feel safe, seen, loved, and cared for."

Lowen's eyes sparkled. "I want to meet Terri one day," he said.

"Me too!" chimed in Aspen and Lowen, her tiny voice full of excitement.

Britney laughed softly. "I hope you can, my loves. Terri has been like a lighthouse guiding me through stormy seas."

"Does Terri know how much you love her?" Harrison asked.

"I think she does," Britney said, her voice filled with emotion. "She's been my therapist, my healer, a lighthouse guiding me safely through every storm. Because of her, I've learned to be that light for myself and all the little parts inside me … and I want to share that light with you."

"Terri gave me the moon so my parts feel safe and connected to her, and now I'm sharing it with you. Remember, whenever you feel scared or lonely, look at the moon and know that my love will always be shining down on you."

A Note from the Author

This story is a piece of my heart, reflecting the journey I've walked with my therapist, Terri, over the last few years. Together, we've explored the many parts within me—the ones that hold joy, fear, sadness, and hope. Terri has been there to guide me, much like a lighthouse on the shore, showing me the way through the foggy waters of my inner world. She has taught me how to listen to these parts, to hold them close, and to show them love when they feel scared or lost.

Through our work, Terri has changed my life in ways I never thought possible. She has helped my inner parts feel safe, loved, and cared for. She gave me the moon as a reminder that no matter the distance, our connection and love remain. It has been a symbol of comfort and love, carrying me through the moments when things felt impossible. Just as a lighthouse's beam cuts through the night, the moon's gentle glow has guided me through the darkness.

This story commemorates the five years of healing together, a journey of finding light in the shadows and learning to embrace every part of myself. And though our time in therapy may one day come to an end, the moon will carry on, shining its light to remind me that I am never truly alone and that our connection will always be in my heart, and I will be in hers.

"Under the moon, I find my way,

a light that guides when skies turn gray.

lighthouse beams and moonlit skies,

hold the parts where love resides."

I hope that by sharing this story, it may inspire others to look within and offer kindness to those hidden, forgotten, and lost parts inside. Healing is a journey, sometimes difficult, but always worth taking. This story is dedicated to Terri and to our continued journey, wherever it may lead.

Britney Shawstad.

Summary

"The Moon That Holds Us" is a heartfelt children's story that gently introduces the concept of internal family systems, showing how both adults and children have different parts inside them that need care and understanding. Through the loving relationship between Britney and her therapist, Terri, the story explores how therapy can help us learn to care for our inner selves. Using the moon as a symbol of connection and comfort, this book offers a tender and accessible way for children to understand complex emotions and the importance of feeling safe and loved, even when things feel hard. It's a story about finding light in the dark, embracing every part of ourselves, and knowing that love is always within reach.

Main Lessons from the Story

1. We All Have Parts Inside Us: The story illustrates that everyone, both children and adults, has different "parts" inside them. These parts represent different feelings and experiences—happiness, sadness, fear, and bravery. It's important to recognize these parts and understand that it's okay to have a mix of feelings inside us.

2. The Role of Therapy: Therapy is portrayed as a safe space where one can learn to listen to and care for their inner parts. Through my relationship with my therapist, Terri, children, and adults can see that seeking help is a kind and courageous act. It's a place to explore our feelings, to learn, and to grow.

3. Connection Beyond Distance: The moon serves as a powerful symbol of connection. It shows that love and support can remain constant, even when we're apart from those we care about. This teaches children that they can carry the love and comfort of others with them, no matter the distance.

4. Caring for Ourselves: I learn to hold my inner parts close, to listen to them, and to offer them love and care. This is a key lesson in self-compassion—it's important to care for our inner selves just as we care for others. When we feel upset, it's our job to listen to those feelings and nurture them.

5. Finding Light in the Darkness: Through the metaphor of the moon and the lighthouse, the story conveys that even in moments of darkness or uncertainty, there is always light to guide us. This teaches children that it's okay to have tough feelings and that hope and comfort can be found, even in the hardest times.

6. The Journey of Healing: The story underscores that healing is a journey. It's not always easy, but it's filled with moments of learning, growth, and connection. By showing Britney's ongoing journey, the story imparts the lesson that healing takes time and that it is a process of embracing all parts of ourselves.

7. The Power of Love and Connection: Ultimately, "The Moon We Share" is about the enduring power of love and connection. It's about how the bonds we share with others can bring comfort and light into our lives, guiding us through difficult times and helping us feel safe and held.

This story is meant to open up conversations about emotions, therapy, and self-care in a way that's gentle and accessible for children. It invites readers to explore their own inner worlds and to find comfort in the idea that they are never alone in their feelings.

www.ingramcontent.com/pod-product-compliance
Lightning Source LLC
Chambersburg PA
CBRC100821120626
46547CB00010B/686